KIM'S
CONVENIENCE

Also by Ins Choi

Subway Stations of the Cross
(Illustrated by Guno Park)

KIM'S
CONVENIENCE

Ins Choi

ANANSI

First edition published in 2012 by House of Anansi Press Inc.

This edition published in 2016 by House of Anansi Press Inc.
houseofanansi.com

House of Anansi Press is committed to protecting our natural environment.
This book is made of material from well-managed FSC®-certified forests,
recycled materials, and other controlled sources.

House of Anansi Press is a Global Certified Accessible™ (GCA by Benetech) publisher. The
ebook version of this book meets stringent accessibility standards and is available to readers
with print disabilities.

27 26 25 24 23   9 10 11 12 13

Library and Archives Canada Cataloguing in Publication

Choi, Ins, 1974–, author
Kim's Convenience / Ins Choi.

Originally published: Toronto : Anansi, 2012.
A play.
ISBN 978-1-4870-0223-7 (paperback)

1. Korean Canadians—Ontario—Toronto—Drama. I. Title.

PS8605.H63K54 2016   C812'.6   C2016-905476-4

Library of Congress Control Number: 2016950152

Text design and Typesetting: Sari Naworynski

*House of Anansi Press is grateful for the privilege to work on and create from the Traditional
Territory of many Nations, including the Anishinabeg, the Wendat, and the Haudenosaunee, as
well as the Treaty Lands of the Mississaugas of the Credit.*

*We acknowledge for their financial support of our publishing program
the Canada Council for the Arts, the Ontario Arts Council, and the Government of Canada.*

Printed and bound in Canada

CONTENTS

CONTENTS

AUTHOR'S NOTE

My father grew up in North Korea. From the time of his birth until the end of the Second World War, the country was occupied by the Japanese. Soon after the Second World War, the Korean Civil War broke out. During that time, he and his family walked south, across the mountainous Korean peninsula, with thousands of others in search of freedom. My mother grew up in an orphanage in war-torn South Korea, raising her younger brother from the age of five. After graduating from high school, she worked as a secretary for the government, at which time she met my father. They arrived in Canada in 1975 with two hundred dollars, three kids, and a lot of hope. My father worked at my uncle's convenience store by day and went to ESL classes by night, while my mother took care of me and my two older sisters.

After a performance of *Kim's Convenience* at the 2011 Toronto Fringe Festival, my parents came up to me, hugged me, and said, "We are very proud of you. Thank you."

Kim's Convenience is my love letter to my parents and to all first-generation immigrants who call Canada their home.

FOREWORD

Two years ago I had a very important conversation with Ins Choi, who had proven himself in the previous year to be a gifted actor — who was also a gifted musician, who was also a gifted poet. No one yet knew that Ins was also a playwright. He was halfway through a two-year residency as a member of the Academy at the Soulpepper Theatre Company, where I am artistic director. The conversation was about life choices, and particularly about one that Ins was not sure he could make: dedicating himself to an artistic life. Ins had been to a family funeral recently and had had a conversation with a policeman friend who had nearly convinced Ins that the steady employment, pension, and community status of an officer of the law were just the answer to his future.

For Ins, it was much more difficult to choose an artistic life than it was for others in the Academy. He arrived in this country from South Korea as a very young child, and grew up in a tight-knit Korean community with a pastor father and an extended family that did not include professional actors or poets or musicians or playwrights. I don't remember exactly what I said during our discussion, but I know the gist: You have great talent; there are so many opportunities in front of you right now; give it at least another year. Six months later, I was handed the first draft of *Kim's Convenience*. A year later, I am writing a Foreword to a play that is now breaking box-office records at Soulpepper, where it launched our fifteenth-anniversary season.

Kim's Convenience is an astonishing debut play. That said, there is nothing original about the form of this play (it does not stray far from the neoclassical unities of time, place, and action) and its subject matter is extremely familiar (literally). What is remarkable about the play is that despite this familiarity, it feels so original. And it feels *very* Canadian. Ins has managed to take the most mundane (dare I say, convenient) institution of our daily life and show us its beating heart. For anyone who has watched this play, it will be impossible to pick up a litre of milk at the corner store without wondering what story is unfolding behind the cash register. Every time we hear the electronic doorbell announcing our departure, we will think about the lives we have left behind.

Kim's Convenience is a textbook example of Mark Twain's maxim, "Write what you know." Ins has written from a very personal and specific place, giving us a picture of one family in one community. The magic depth to which he has taken this specificity is the same depth from which the play's universality is sprung. This play, on hearing, becomes *our* story about *our* family in *our* community.

As a classical actor, Ins has been around great plays and he has learned from them. We feel the ghosts of Willy and Biff Loman in this play, and it is interesting to note that Ins was rehearsing and performing *Death of a Salesman* while writing

Kim's Convenience. Ins' ability to capture cadence and humour reminds us of the great Mercer family trilogy of David French.

But the play that *Kim's Convenience* reminds me of the most is Lorraine Hansberry's *A Raisin in the Sun*. Like Hansberry's breakthrough play, *Kim's Convenience* arrives as both an artistic triumph and a major cultural event. Ins Choi has opened a door through which many will follow. Ten years from now there will be a new generation of first- and second-generation Canadians who will know, with confidence, that they can make a meaningful contribution to the well-being of their community without a uniform and a gun. For many of this generation, the first step of that journey to cultural confidence will be through the door that Ins Choi has opened. (*Cue sound of doorbell*)

Albert Schultz
Artistic Director
Soulpepper Theatre Company
Toronto, Ontario
February 2012

INTRODUCTION

In the late nineteenth century, Canadian missionaries began working in South Korea. They built churches, hospitals, schools, and universities, while developing close relationships with the people. In 1948, a mission-sponsored medical student named Tae-Yon Whang arrived in Canada to continue his studies. After completing his education, he decided to stay and inadvertently became the first Korean to officially immigrate to Canada.

In 1965, there were seventy Korean immigrants in Canada. In 1967, the first Korean church was established at St. Luke's United Church on the corner of Sherbourne Street and Carlton Street in downtown Toronto. Originally named the Toronto Korean Church, it was renamed the Toronto Korean United Church after becoming a part of the United Church of Canada. In 1973, the Ontario Korean Businessmen's Association (OKBA) was established. The organization offered group purchasing to small businesses through its wholesale outlet and serviced mainly Korean convenience store owners.

With the Korean church and the OKBA established, Koreans could come to Toronto, make friends, gain support, purchase a store, fill the store with products, and make a pretty good living without ever having to learn English. Korean convenience stores spread all over Toronto, as did the Korean churches. In 1980 there were 20,000 Koreans in Canada, and in 2011 that number rose to 200,000. I've always considered the church and the store to be the *Umma* and the *Appa* of Korean communities in Canada.

When I graduated from the acting program at York University in 1998, there were few Asian actors to look up to. In fact, there was a lack of roles for Asian males in plays, TV shows, and movies. The only roles out there were two-bit parts in three-bit movies-of-the-week, involving silent-on-camera Asian gang members. Was this my career? There were the plays of Rick Shiomi, Jean Yoon, Marty Chan, and M. J. Kang, which inspired me, but that was about it. Something needed to change.

Then, in 2002, fu-GEN Asian Canadian Theatre Company was launched under the leadership of Nina Lee Aquino, Richard Lee, David Yee, and Leon Aureus. Through fu-GEN, the Asian theatre community in Toronto was being nurtured, award-winning shows were being produced, and new plays were being written. In 2005, Nina invited me to be part of their third playwriting unit. That was the beginning of *Kim's Convenience*. Over the next five years, I received writing grants from the Ontario Arts Council and the Toronto Arts Council, and was given workshop opportunities to finish this play from fu-GEN, Diaspora Dialogues, and Grace Toronto Church. It was a gruelling process. I gave up many times and celebrated the work's completion on countless occasions. And although I didn't think the play was finished, in 2010 I submitted it to a few theatre companies in Toronto, just to see what feedback I'd receive. All of them were encouraging, but none of them were interested. It was then that I realized I would have to birth this play myself. In my research of independent theatre festivals in Toronto, I came across the New Play Contest held by the Toronto Fringe Festival. The winner would automatically have his or her show in the festival, the eight-hundred-dollar entrance fee would be waived, and the title "Winner of New Play Contest" would be plastered all over promotional materials. I entered. It won.

Renowned theatre director Weyni Mengesha had agreed to direct the show, but due to scheduling conflicts she couldn't. So I took on the Herculean task of producing and directing the play I had written, which I was also performing in. I had no money, so I began raising funds through donations from friends and family, and selling ad space in the playbill. Soon after, actor and playwright Leon Aureus came on board as co-producer. We knew that we could count on the Toronto theatre-going crowd because of the quality of the cast and because the play had won the New Play Contest. What would prove to be a challenge was reaching the Korean audience, which was vital to me.

We went to every Korean store in K-town south (Christie and Bloor) and K-town north (Yonge and Finch), putting up posters and talking up the show. We sent posters with a cover letter to every Korean church in Toronto. We were interviewed by all the Korean media outlets and even ran a "Win Free Tickets: Korean Trivia Contest" through our Facebook page. Leon posted trailers on YouTube, which a lot of the Korean media picked up and ran on their programs. Later, Sojeong Choi came on board and did an incredible job in helping us publicize the play to the Korean community. Even cast members were tweeting, posting on Facebook, doing whatever they could to help the show gain exposure. That was the producing side of it. That was the hard part.

The show itself proved to be the easy part. I already had the cast in mind from doing workshops in the past, and they were all willing to be in the play for pretty much nothing. Actors Paul Sun-Hyung Lee, Jean Yoon, Esther Jun, André Sills, and I, along with stage manager Kat Chin and designer Ken Mackenzie, met whenever we could, rehearsing free of charge in the basement of Grace Toronto Church and in the sanctuary of Toronto Korean Bethel Church. Rehearsals were highly collaborative. We ate out together a lot and got to know each other very well.

By the time we opened, all of the advance tickets (50 percent of the run) had been sold and there was an incredible, euphoric buzz surrounding the show, especially after it had been featured on the cover of *NOW Magazine*. People were lining up for tickets two to three hours in advance and many were turned away. One Korean family came all the way from Parry Sound at the request of their friends, who told them to "Close the store and come see this play; it's about us." The audience was about one-third Korean, one-third Caucasian, and one-third every other ethnicity under the sun, young and old. All seven performances at the two-hundred-seat Bathurst Street Theatre had sold out. The play then went on to win the Patron's Pick Award, selling out an additional show in three hours. It was invited to be part of the Best of Fringe Uptown Festival, where it sold out an additional seven shows at the two-hundred-seat Studio Theatre at the Toronto Centre for the Arts.

It was then that I began receiving emails from commercial producers and artistic directors of Toronto theatre companies, who were interested in mounting my play. Soulpepper was the best fit. Soulpepper's founder and artistic director, Albert Schultz, wanted the play to open the company's 2012 season. Everybody was available except André Sills, who had to honour a previous contract for another show. So we auditioned all the available amazing black actors in Toronto and arrived at Clé Bennett. When I was asked about a director, I immediately proposed Weyni. This time, her schedule was open.

On December 19, 2011, we began rehearsals for *Kim's Convenience* at Soulpepper Theatre Company. Weyni began with a ritual: each of us would share a personal object and the story of what had got us into theatre. (Those objects are hidden in our set.) We rehearsed six days a week, eight hours a day, for three weeks. Every Wednesday night, we ate Korean, Ethiopian, or Jamaican cuisine, and on Saturdays we brought sweet treats to the rehearsals. The show opened at Soulpepper on January 19, 2012.

It's Thursday, February 2, 2012, 7:30 p.m. I'm sitting on a couch in the green room at Soulpepper Theatre. Nancy, the stage manager, just gave us the thirty-minute call. I'm tired . . . I should get ready . . . Paul Sun-Hyung Lee, who plays Appa in the show, is sitting beside me playing some game on his iPad. Esther Jun, who plays Janet, walked in and asked something about hosting our closing-night party. Jean Yoon, who plays Umma, just sat down. Actor Clé Bennett, who plays four roles in the show, came in and dropped a bunch of sweet potato chips that he discovered recently and which we all love. (Everybody gets up to hug Clé. He just brings that out in all of us.) Natalie, the dresser, is doing a crossword puzzle at the table. Kat, the assistant stage manager, walked by tweeting something. Nancy is now knitting a baby blanket for the soon-to-be-born baby of Ken Mackenzie, the set designer. Everyone has now vacated the room to get ready for the show . . . I'm alone in this room writing on my laptop now. I've been alone in some room writing on my laptop for the past six years, dreaming of this. Chipping away at this unrelenting script, wrestling with these characters, laughing and weeping as I find myself in the story, can't help but feel sad knowing that the Kim's Convenience *file titles on my laptop end here.*

kc.2006.05.FinalDraft2.cwk
kc.2006.fugenPotluck.cwk
kc1.2007.now.cwk
kc2.2007.09.27.DiasporaDialogues.cwk
kc3.2008.06.28.fugen.megapotluck.cwk
kc5.2009.04.22.cwk
kc6.2009.05.20.GraceChurch.cwk
kc.2010.Autumn.Fringe.NewPlayContest.pdf
kc.2011.04.01.Fringe.cwk
kc.2011.07.03.Fringe.cwk
kc.2011.12.07.soulpepper.postreading.rtf
kc.2012.01.12.soulpepper.rtf
kc.2012.02.11.anansi.doc

In our opening week, Kim's Convenience *sold out its entire thirty-eight–show run in the two-hundred-seat Michael Young Theatre. Soulpepper is bringing the show back in May, and we plan to tour it across Canada and around the world . . . honoured and humbled. As if a pack of wild rhinos trampled a path before me, knocking down all the barriers and smoothing every rocky place . . . I should get ready . . . Not many people in the arts have faith in God anymore. But I do and I thank God for having faith in me. Enough faith to let me play . . . I should get ready . . .*

Ins Choi
Toronto, Ontario
February 2012

KIM'S CONVENIENCE
김씨네 편의점

Kim's Convenience made its debut at the 2011 Toronto Fringe Festival, where it was first performed on July 6, 2011, at the Bathurst Street Theatre. The play was revived in Toronto on January 19, 2012, by the Soulpepper Theatre Company at the Young Centre for the Performing Arts. The original cast members are:

APPA	Paul Sun-Hyung Lee
UMMA	Jean Yoon
JUNG	Ins Choi
JANET	Esther Jun

RICH, MR. LEE,	Andre Sills (Fringe Festival production)
MIKE, and ALEX	Clé Bennett (Soulpepper Theatre production)

Fringe Festival production directed by Ins Choi
Soulpepper Theatre production directed by Weyni Mengesha

CHARACTERS

APPA
A 59-year-old first-generation Korean-Canadian man,
and owner of Kim's Convenience store.
Speaks with a thick Korean-Canadian accent.

UMMA
A 56-year-old first-generation Korean-Canadian woman.
APPA's wife. Speaks with a thick Korean-Canadian accent.

JUNG
A 32-year-old second-generation Korean-Canadian man.
APPA and UMMA's son.

JANET
A 30-year-old second-generation Korean-Canadian woman.
APPA and UMMA's daughter.

The following characters are played by one actor:

RICH
A young black man

MR. LEE
A successful black real estate agent and a friend of APPA

MIKE
A black man with a thick Jamaican accent

ALEX
A 32-year-old black police officer and a childhood
friend of JUNG

SCENE

A convenience store in Toronto's Regent Park,
a low- to middle-income neighbourhood
made up mainly of recent immigrants.

1. Open

Autumn. Morning. Inside a convenience store.

APPA *is heard humming a medley of hymns as he enters from the back of the store with a pocketful of money, a mug of coffee in hand, and scratch-and-win card trays. He puts the coffee mug on the counter, inserts the money in the cash register, and slides in the scratch-and-win trays. He turns on the lights, then goes to the window and flips the CLOSED sign to OPEN. He unlocks the front door. He returns to the counter, pours sugar in his coffee, and stirs. As he looks out the window, he sips. He sighs. He turns on the radio and begins pricing a case of cans with a price gun.*

2. I am Korean

Early afternoon. Bell. RICH enters.

APPA: Hi.

RICH: Hey, wassup?

APPA: Nice day.

RICH: Yeah. Hook me up with a scratch-and-win card, please? (*APPA pulls out the tray and* RICH *chooses a card.*) Thanks.

APPA: Is that one you car?

RICH: Sorry?

APPA: *Pointing to a car outside.* Is that one you car?

RICH: Is that one my car?

APPA: Yah.

RICH: Which one?

APPA: White Honda in no-parking zone. Is that one you car?

RICH: No, man, I don't even have a car.

APPA: Oh.

RICH: And a du Maurier Balanced, please.

APPA: Large or small?

RICH: Small.

APPA: King size or regular?

RICH: King size.

APPA: If you don't have car, why you ask, "Which one?" when I ask, "Is that one you car?"

RICH: I don't know. Didn't know what you were talking about.

APPA: *Indicating the case of cans on the counter.* Insam Energy Beverage?

RICH: What?

APPA: It's Insam Energy Beverage. It's new one, very good from Korea. Made from —

RICH: Ginseng.

APPA: No, insam.

RICH: No, like what it's made from, looks like ginseng.

APPA: No, looks like insam. That's why it's call —

23

RICH: You're not hearing me. (*Picking up a can.*) The picture, right here, it's ginseng.

APPA: No, picture is insam.

RICH: Yo — forget it, it's no big deal. (*Putting the can back.*)

APPA: Yo, it's very big deal. Look same, not same thing. 1904. You know what happen 1904? Japan attack Korea.

RICH: Japan attacked Korea?

APPA: Yah.

RICH: In 1904?

APPA: Yah.

RICH: Are you Japanese?

APPA: No.

RICH: You look Japanese.

APPA: No.

RICH: Yo, you look like that guy in *The Last Samurai*.

APPA: Who, Tom Cruise?

RICH: No, the Japanese guy.

APPA: Look same, not same thing. You look like you is from Kenya.

RICH: I am from Kenya. I was born there. How'd you know that?

APPA: I can tell.

RICH: Really?

APPA: Yeah. Really.

RICH: Yo, that is cool.

APPA: I know. I am.

RICH: Why were we talking about Japan attacking Korea?

APPA: Japan attack Korea 1904, make slave of Korean. I am Korean. Ginseng is Japanese name. Insam is Korean name. (*Beat.*) Look same —

APPA &
RICH: — not same thing.

APPA: You understand.

RICH: Yeah, I gotcha. Hook me up.

APPA: Okay. I hook up. Anything else?

RICH: No, that's it.

APPA: *Tallies up the total on the cash register.* $12.52.

       RICH *gives* APPA *a twenty.*

RICH: Thanks.

       APPA *gives* RICH *his change.*

APPA: Okay. See you.

       RICH *remains at the counter and plays the scratch-and-win card. He loses.*

APPA: You win?

RICH: Nah.

APPA: You choose bad one. Okay, see you.

RICH: Yeah, have a good one.

       RICH *exits. Bell.*

3. Call police

       JANET *enters from the back of the store with her camera bag. She goes to the side closet for her jacket and fills up on candy throughout the scene.*

APPA: Janet.

JANET: Bye Appa.

APPA: Call police.

JANET: *Startled.* What happened?

APPA: Car is no-parking zone. (*Offers her the cordless phone.*) Call police.

JANET: I gotta go.

APPA: *Slowly dialling.* Nine . . . one —

JANET: Stop being so nosy.

APPA: YOU nosy! Talk to police.

JANET: I'm not talking to the police.

APPA: I'm push last one.

JANET: I don't care if you push last one. I'm not talking to the police.

APPA: I don't care if you don't care, I'm push last one.

JANET: Mind your own business, Appa.

APPA: This is my business. Talk to police.

27

JANET: What, it's a Toyota?

APPA: No.

JANET: Mitsubishi?

APPA: No. (*Beat.*) Okay, it's Honda, but still —

JANET: How many times do I have to tell you, Appa, Japanese people aren't the only ones driving Japanese cars.

APPA: You buy Japanese, you is guilty by associationship.

JANET: What about your Canon SLR camera, made in Japan?

APPA: Appa get half-price.

JANET: Your money still went to Japan.

APPA: Half-price, I rip off Japan.

JANET: Still Japanese.

APPA: I scratch name. Nobody can tell. Talk to police.

JANET: What about Mr. Shin? He's a salesman for Honda.

APPA: Mr. Shin is Mr. Shit.

JANET: I thought you guys were best friends?

APPA: No, he is pimping the Jesus now.

JANET: What?

APPA: He is pimping the Jesus.

JANET: He's doing what to Jesus?

APPA: Pimping.

JANET: Peemping?

APPA: Not peemping, pimping.

JANET: Pimping.

APPA: Yah. He is using church to selling Honda. Different
         church every Sunday, selling Honda. That's pimping
         the Jesus.

JANET: How'd you learn about a word like pimping?

APPA: Janet, I am cool, what you talking?

JANET: Okay, what about Mr. Park? He sets up cheap sushi
         restaurants in the Annex. He's promoting Japanese
         cuisine. He's guilty by associationship, and since
         you're his best friend, so are you.

APPA: No.

JANET: Yes.

APPA: No.

JANET: Yes.

APPA: No. That's different. He is pimping Japan. Pimping
        Japan is okay. He is make money selling Japan food,
        but he is Korean. White people can't tell difference.
        Kind of look same. Korean Grill House, run by
        Chinese. Chinese pimping Korea. That's no good.
        Appa boycott. Talk to police.

JANET: Talk to them yourself.

APPA: Police hear accent, they don't take serious.

JANET: Appa —

APPA: Janet! 1904 Japan attack Korea —

        Bell. MR. LEE, *a successful real estate agent, enters.*

JANET: Okay, fine! I'll call the police.

APPA: 그래! 아이씨 참! [That's right!]

        JANET *takes out her cellphone.*

—
30

4. The offer

LEE: Mr. Kim.

APPA: Oh, Mr. Lee! My black friend with Korean last name!

LEE: Hi Janet.

JANET: Hey, Mr. Lee.

JANET exits. Bell.

APPA: Long time now see.

LEE: Yeah, it's been a while.

APPA: Wah, look at you, nice jacket, pants. Turn around. Turn around. (*LEE does a flashy Michael Jackson turn.*) Wah, looks very good.

LEE: You like this? I can get you one.

APPA: Oh, no, no thank you. Not my style. How's mommy, daddy?

LEE: They're doing very well, thank you.

APPA: And how's you business?

LEE: Business is good. Business is very good. (*Beat.*

Gazing out the window.) Lotta condos going up in the area, eh, Mr. Kim?

APPA: Yah, very fast. They is working hard.

LEE: Did you hear about Walmart?

APPA: Walmart? What's Walmart?

LEE: Apparently once those condos are up and ready, Walmart's moving in.

APPA: Why Walmart wants to moving to Regent Park?

LEE: 'Cuz once those condos are up and ready, Regent Park isn't gonna be Regent Park anymore. (*LEE hands APPA his card.*) Here.

APPA: I already have you card.

LEE: This is a new one. Flip it over.

APPA: What flip?

LEE: The card. Flip the card over, Mr. Kim. (*APPA turns the card upside down.*) That's not a flip, that's a turn.

APPA: Oh, flip, okay.

APPA flips the card over twice.

LEE: You're back on the same — just — I'm serious, Mr. Kim! (*LEE grabs APPA's hands, showing him the back of the card.*) There. See?

APPA: No, I can't see. Light is no good here. (*APPA goes back behind the counter.*) What is?

LEE: That's my offer for your store, Mr. Kim.

APPA: Offer?

LEE: Mr. Kim, I want to purchase your store.

APPA: You want to buy my store?

LEE: Yes, I want to buy your store for that amount.

APPA: Oh, Mr. Lee, this is lots of money.

LEE: I wouldn't dare insult you with anything less.

Beat.

APPA: This is very generous, Mr. Lee, but, no. This community need me. Even if Walmart moving in, people in neighbourhood need this store.

LEE: I understand that, Mr. Kim, but once Walmart moves in, I'm sorry to say, but that's it. No one can compete with that kinda buying power. Dufferin Mall, Jane and St. Clair —

APPA: Mr. Lee, my answer is no! Thank you.

APPA offers the card. LEE takes the card and resolves to leave.

LEE: Mr. Kim, do you have an exit plan?

APPA: Exit plan?

LEE: What's your exit plan, Mr. Kim? What's your exit plan from this life? You plan on working at the store 'til you die? That's not a good exit plan. You've had a rough life, especially with your son. Don't think for a minute that I don't remember the kind of trouble Jung put you through. Now if Jung were here, he'd take over the store. But he's not here and he's not coming back. (*Offering his card.*) This is your only opportunity to enjoy life a little, Mr. Kim, before there's only a little life left to enjoy. (APPA *doesn't take the card. LEE puts it on the counter.*) Well, think it over. Give me a call tonight. I gotta go. I'm parked in a no-parking zone.

Bell. JANET enters.

JANET: Appa, did you see my Day-timer?

APPA: Mr. Lee! (*JANET puts her bags on the counter and rushes into the side closet.*) White Honda is you car?

LEE: Yeah. Mr. Shin gave me an offer I couldn't refuse. Give me a call.

34

Bell. LEE exits. APPA takes out a printing calculator and adds up some figures. He tears off the receipt and looks at it close up. It's impressive. He puts LEE's card on the cash register and begins making a list of things to pick up at the wholesaler.

5. I am serious

JANET is in the side closet looking for her Day-timer.

APPA: Janet?

JANET: What?

APPA: Did you call police?

JANET: Yeah.

APPA: Good. Now, call police again and cancel order.

JANET: What?

APPA: Cancel order, we don't need.

JANET: Forget it. You cancel the order.

APPA: I am serious, Janet.

JANET: Seriously?

APPA: Yah, seriously.

JANET: No kidding?

APPA: No kidding.

JANET: You serious?

APPA: Yah, I am serious.

JANET: No foolin'?

APPA: Who is fooling?

JANET: You.

APPA: No. What you talking?

JANET: I'm talking serious.

JANET appears.

APPA: Me too.

JANET: You don't look serious.

APPA: My face is serious.

JANET: That's your serious face?

APPA: This is my serious face!

JANET: Seriously?

APPA: Seriously!!

UMMA enters with her jacket on, carrying her purse and a covered tray of food.

UMMA: *To APPA.* 그만해 아이씨참!! [Will you two quit it!!]

JANET, with a mischievous smile, exits to the back of the store.

APPA restocks the gum shelf as UMMA puts the tray of food behind the counter.

6. I'm going

UMMA: 내가 이따가 와서 치울께요. [Just leave it, I'll clean it up when I get back.]

APPA: 주일날 최집사님이 저녁 같이 하자네. 시간돼? [This Sunday Mr. Chae wants to get together for dinner. How's your schedule?]

UMMA: *Picking up LEE's card.* 이게 뭐에요? [What's this?]

APPA: 어 ... 그거 ... 그러니까 그게 ... Mr. Lee 가 오퍼 넌거야 ... 우리가게. [Oh ... that's, uh ... Mr. Lee's offer ... for the store.]

UMMA: 오퍼요? 가게 판다는 얘기 안했잖아요. [I didn't know you were selling the store.]

APPA: 팔려고 하는게 아니라 ... Mr.Lee 방금 오퍼를 상의 도 없이 주고 갔데니까. [I wasn't ... Mr. Lee just made an offer. Just now.]

UMMA: 가격은 꽤 괜찮네. [It's a generous offer.]

APPA: 그러게 ... [I know ...]

UMMA: 은퇴할 수 있겠네. [You could retire.]

APPA: 그러게. [I know.]

UMMA: *Beat. Gets herself together.* Janet, I'm going. Janet, I'm going to church. Janet? Janet!

JANET appears.

JANET: What?!

UMMA: 엄마 갔다올께. [I'm going to church.]

JANET: Then 가 [go] already.

UMMA: *Under her breath as she leaves.* 아휴, 이 기집애 때매 내가 죽겠다, 죽겠어. [Ugh, I swear, she's gonna be the death of me, the death of me.]

UMMA exits. Bell.

7. What's your plan?

APPA resumes pricing the cans. JANET is organizing her camera lenses and lens-cleaning materials at the counter.

APPA: Janet.

JANET: What, Appa, she drives me crazy!

APPA: Do you have exit plan?

JANET: What?

APPA: Do you have exit plan?

JANET: Do I have a what?

          APPA stops pricing.

APPA: Exit plan. You having?

JANET: An exit plan? For what?

APPA: No, like what's you life plan?

JANET: What are you talking about?

APPA: You is thirty years old now. Have to think what is plan you future. What you think, take over store?

JANET: I don't want to work at the store.

APPA: What's wrong with store?

JANET: How can I work at the store, Appa? I'm busy.

APPA: Not work at store. I am talking take over store.
        Make Kim's Convenience dynasty.

JANET: Take over the store?

APPA: Yah.

JANET: Don't you want me to succeed in life? Look, Appa,
        you did what you had to do, right? And I appreciate
        that. I do. But didn't you do what you had to do so I
        wouldn't have to do what I had to do but could
        choose what I wanted to do?

APPA: What?

JANET: I'm a photographer, Appa. This is what I've chosen
        to do.

APPA: Yah, you can do weekend. Hobby, like me. But you
        don't make money take picture. Store make money.
        Take over store: money. Picture: hobby. It's good
        deal for you.

JANET: I don't want to take over the store. I don't even know
        how to run the store.

        JANET goes back into the closet.

8. Jamaican

> *Bell.* MIKE *enters. He speaks with a thick Jamaican accent.*

MIKE: Hey, man, wa gwan? D'ya have a tub o' Vaseline fa me? A tub o' Vaseline?

> *Beat.*

APPA: What?

MIKE: D'ya have a tub o' Vaseline?

APPA: Seen? Sorry, I don't — I can't catch fast what you talking.

> *Beat.*

MIKE: What?

APPA: I can't catch hearing you speak mouth too fast.

MIKE: What ya talking about?

APPA: No, uh, what you talking?

MIKE: About what?

APPA: What?

MIKE: What what?

APPA: No, you ask me —

MIKE: Y'aks me what I talking, what ya referring to?

APPA: Why you talking like you want to fight me?

MIKE: Me not speaking like me want to fight ya. Me not
          want to fight. Me just need a tub o' Vaseline, see,
          and dis how me speak, take it or leave it.

APPA: Okay, I take.

MIKE: Ladda mercy, me look for it me damn self. Cha!
          (*As he walks down an aisle*) Chinaman wan run
          business in Canada and him can't even speak da
          language proply.

9. Steal or no steal

          *JANET appears and APPA ushers her behind the coun-
          ter at the window.*

APPA: Janet, Janet, you see?

JANET: See what?

APPA: That guy.

JANET: Which guy?

APPA: Not front of store, back of store. See? Don't look! See, but don't look.

JANET: The black guy?

APPA: Janet, don't be racist.

JANET: What?

APPA: You see?

JANET: Yeah, I saw the guy. So?

APPA: He is steal.

JANET: What?

APPA: He is steal.

JANET: You saw him take something?

APPA: No, he is going to steal.

JANET: How can you tell?

APPA: He is black guy, jean jacket. That combo is steal combo. You don't know how to run store, I teach you. This is training day. Lesson number one, steal or no steal. Every customer, have to know. Steal or no steal. (*Beat. Pointing to a girl outside.*) See that girl? She is no steal. She is black girl, fat. Fat black girl is no steal. (*Pointing to a guy outside.*) Fat white guy, that's steal. Fat guy is black, brown shoes, that's no steal. That's cancel-out combo.

JANET: That is so awkwardly racist.

APPA: Not racist . . . survival skill. Look. Secret survival skill. (*Closes his eyes and looks around.*) Make eyes very small. Then nobody know you even looking. (*Reopens his eyes.*) Okay, brown guy, that's steal. Brown girl, that's no steal. Asian guy, that's no steal. Asian girl, that's steal. If you is the gay, that's no steal. Easy. The gay is never steal. If you is the lesbian, that is girl who is the gay, that's steal, one hundred percent guarantee they is steal. But two lesbian, that's no steal, cancel-out combo.

JANET: What about a black lesbian with long straight hair and a fat Asian gay man with short hair together? Steal or no steal?

APPA: That's impossible.

JANET: What's impossible?

APPA: The gay, Asian, fat?

JANET: Appa, there are Asians who are gay, y'know?

APPA: I know, but the gay Asian is never fat. Only skinny Asian is the gay. That's rule. Shhh.

10. Hapkido

MIKE: Me find it in da back.

MIKE comes to the counter with a tub of Vaseline.

APPA: Oh, Vaseline. You using for feet? I using for feet. My heel get hard and cracking. Vaseline make smooth.

MIKE: Right.

APPA: *Tallies up the total on the cash register.* $4.65. (*MIKE gives APPA a twenty.*) Thank you. Okay, I give to you change.

APPA closes the cash register and comes around to the other side of the counter, standing between MIKE and the door.

MIKE: Wa gwan?

APPA: I have you change here my hand. I give to you change, you give to me what you steal.

JANET: Appa!

MIKE: What?!

APPA: Give to me what you steal, I give to you change.

JANET: Appa!

MIKE: 'Cuz me black, y'accusing me of teefin'?

JANET: No! I'm sorry, sir —

APPA: *To JANET.* Janet, stay back. (*To MIKE*) No, I'm not accuse you. I'm tell you, you is steal.

JANET: *Coming forward.* Appa, stop it! (*To MIKE*) Sorry, he's got a weird sense of —

APPA: Janet! (*JANET moves.*) Give to me what you steal from back of store and I give to you change.

MIKE: Excuse me, but —

APPA: No, I don't excuse you. You have no excuse. You living in Canada, you is healthy, you is smart, you is good boy, you have no excuse to steal.

MIKE: Ya making big mistake —

JANET picks up the phone.

APPA: No, you making big mistake. I know hapkido. You know hapkido? It's Korean fighting style. That's big mistake for you. Now, you want something, you pay. You can pay cash or you can pay I kick you ass.

MIKE attempts to run. APPA grabs his arm, twisting it, sending MIKE to the floor in a submission hold.

MIKE: AH!

APPA: Empty pocket. Empty pocket!

APPA applies pressure to MIKE's arm.

MIKE: AH! (*MIKE takes a pack of razors out of his pocket.*) Please don't hand me over.

APPA: You didn't pay for this.

MIKE: Please, me sorry. (*APPA applies pressure to MIKE's arm.*) AH! Please don't hand me over.

MIKE takes a pack of toothpaste out of his pocket.

APPA: You didn't pay for that.

MIKE: Please.

APPA: "I am steal from you store, Mr. Kim." Repeat. "I am steal from you store, Mr. Kim. Please forgive me." Repeat!

MIKE: I am steal from ya store, Mr. Kim. Please fahgive me.

APPA: "Dear Jesus."

MIKE: What? (*APPA applies pressure to his arm.*) AH!

APPA: Repeat. "Dear Jesus."

MIKE: Dear Jesus.

APPA: "Please forgive me I am steal from Mr. Kim."

MIKE: Please fahgive me I am steal from Mr. Kim.

APPA: "Help me be good example to black kid."

MIKE: Help me be a good example to the black kids them.

APPA: "I accept you in my heart."

MIKE: What? (*APPA applies pressure to his arm.*) AH!

APPA: Repeat!

MIKE: I accept ya in a me heart.

APPA: "Amen."

MIKE: Amen.

APPA: Walk out slow. And if I ever see you, I shit kick you
        fuck ass, you understand?

MIKE: Ya, man.

APPA *lets go.* MIKE *makes to leave.*

APPA: *Getting his attention.* Ya.

      MIKE *turns around.* APPA *tosses him the tub of Vaseline.* MIKE *catches it.*

MIKE: Thank you, Mr. Kim.

      MIKE *walks out. Bell.*

APPA: You not welcome.

11. YOU stupid

APPA: See, I tell you he is steal. (*Picks up the stolen items, putting them on the counter.*) That is lesson number one. Steal or no steal. Have to know. Okay, lesson number two —

JANET: That was the most idiotic, insanely stupid thing I've ever seen you do, and you've done a lot of stupid things, Appa.

APPA: YOU stupid.

JANET: Appa!

APPA: He is stupid too.

JANET: Of course he's stupid! Why else would he be stealing unless he's stupid!

APPA: David Chen, Lucky Moose in Chinatown, do same thing. He is hero. I am hero.

JANET: Kenny Kim, Queen and Sherbourne, did the same thing and it cost him his life.

APPA: Kenny Kim is die because cigarette company and government is so greedy. They make cigarette so expensive, people can't afford and have to steal. Then convenience store owner is victim. That's why Kenny Kim is die. Don't get mix up, Janet.

JANET: Appa, that guy could've had a gun.

APPA: I know hapkido.

JANET: *Picking up the stolen items and placing them behind the counter.* Is it worth it? Is it really worth it? Grow up, Appa!

APPA: YOU grow up.

JANET: Did you even think about —

APPA: YOU think.

JANET: What?

APPA: YOU what.

JANET: Stop doing that!

APPA: YOU stop.

JANET: I'm not doing anything.

APPA: YOU doing.

JANET: I'm just talking.

APPA: YOU talking.

JANET: Appa, that doesn't even make any —

APPA: YOU doesn't.

JANET: You're just repeating —

APPA: YOU.

JANET: Alright!

APPA: YOU alright.

JANET: Fine.

APPA: YOU fine.

JANET: Forget it.

APPA: YOU forget.

Beat.

JANET: Turn.

APPA: YOU turn.

JANET: Niverse.

APPA: YOU niverse.

JANET: Tube.

APPA: YOU tube.

JANET: Calyptus!

Bell. Police officer ALEX enters.

APPA: YOU calyptus!

JANET: Thanasia!

APPA: YOU thanasia!!

JANET: Kulele!!!

APPA: YOU kulele!!!!!

12. Police

ALEX: Excuse me, sir, did someone here call 9-1-1?

APPA: Yah.

ALEX: Who called 9-1-1?

APPA: I do.

ALEX: Is there an emergency? Sir!

APPA: Yah, used be emergency. You take so long time not emergency now.

ALEX: What was the emergency, sir?

APPA: White Honda is parking no-parking zone. Then drive off. You take too long.

ALEX: Sir, 9-1-1 is reserved for emergency situations. Please don't abuse it with trivial matters like illegally parked cars. There are severe consequences —

APPA: Actual, I don't call 9-1-1, Janet is.

JANET: Appa!

ALEX: Is this true, miss?

JANET: Well, yes, Officer, technically —

ALEX: Janet?

JANET: Yes?

ALEX: Planet Janet?

JANET: Alex?

ALEX: Look at you.

JANET: Oh my God, you're a cop.

ALEX: And you're . . . all grown up.

Beat.

APPA: What's happen?

JANET: Appa, this is Alex. He . . . he was a friend of Jung.

ALEX: Hi, Mr. Kim.

APPA: Oh, yah, I remember you, yah. Hi, Alex. (*Beat.*) You is now police?

ALEX: Yeah.

APPA: Real police?

ALEX: What can I say, Mr. Kim. People change. (*ALEX shows APPA his badge.*)

APPA clears his throat and gestures for the badge.
ALEX gives it to APPA. APPA checks to see if it's real
and then returns the badge.

APPA: You daddy must be very proud of you.

ALEX: Yeah, he was. He passed away two years ago, but he was very proud.

APPA: I'm sorry.

ALEX: That's okay.

APPA: How's you mommy?

ALEX: She's good, very busy at church, as usual. Wow, can't believe you guys are still here. Is Jung here?

Beat.

APPA: Alex, you want something drink? Janet, take to back, give him something drink.

ALEX: No, it's okay.

APPA: Not okay.

ALEX: No, I'm fine.

APPA: Not fine.

ALEX: Please —

APPA: Please take something.

ALEX: No, it's really okay, Mr. Kim —

APPA: Not really okay, Alex.

ALEX: Mr. Kim —

APPA: Alex! You in my store, you is my business! Take
drink, give to you energy. (*Gives an insam drink
to him.*) Janet, take to back, give him snack. Police
is hungry job, need energy. (*JANET and ALEX go
to the back of the store.*) Peanuts. Take peanuts.
Peanuts is good snack. Janet, give to him peanuts.
Salty peanuts. Honey-roasted peanuts. Chocolate-
cover peanuts, that's good taste. (*JANET and ALEX
are chuckling.*) It's true.

JANET: Okay, Planters cocktail peanuts. How about a Clif Bar?

APPA: Yah, okay.

JANET: You like Crispers?

APPA: Good.

JANET: Gotta be ranch. Oh, and Pringles, pizza-flavoured.
Definitely a couple of Combos Cheddar Cheese
Pretzels. That's for sure.

APPA: Okay, that's good enough.

JANET: Peek Freans Shortcake. Gatorade Cool Blue.

APPA: Okay, that's last one.

JANET: Hubba Bubba Strawberry —

APPA: Janet!

JANET comes to the front. ALEX has his arms full of stuff.

JANET: What?

APPA: What you doing? He is back to working time is now.

JANET gets ALEX a plastic bag for the snacks.

ALEX: He's right, I gotta go, Janet. This is more than enough. Hey, could I get Jung's number? I'd really like to hook up with him.

APPA: What? Oh, sorry, no, we don't having that kind. Okay, bye, Alex.

ALEX: Yeah. Okay. Bye, Mr. Kim. It was really good seeing you, Janet.

JANET: Yeah, same here.

ALEX: Yeah, me too.

JANET: Yeah.

Beat.

APPA: Okay, bye, Alex, see you.

ALEX exits. Bell. JANET watches ALEX exit.

APPA: *Checking his watch.* Okay, Janet, I have to take big *ddong* now. We continue training after. Watch store.

APPA takes the cordless phone and exits to the back; JANET resumes looking for her Day-timer behind the counter.

13. Where's your brother?

Bell. ALEX enters store.

ALEX: Hi.

JANET: Hi. Did you forget something?

ALEX: No.

JANET: You need more peanuts?

ALEX: *Chuckles.* Wow. No, I have enough. I just wanted to leave my number for Jung. What? What is it?

Beat.

JANET: Guess you guys haven't kept in touch, eh? (*beat*)
He left . . . a long time ago.

ALEX: He left?

JANET: Yeah. He left home when he was sixteen.

ALEX: Didn't know that.

JANET: You remember Jung's temper? My dad was the same.
Even worse.

ALEX: What happened?

JANET: Uh, well, during one of their arguments, Jung said
that Appa was a horrible husband, that he was treat-
ing my mom like a slave. And Appa hit him. Hard.
Jung was hospitalized for a few days. After he was
released, everything seemed to be back to normal.
Then, one day, my dad went to get the money from
the safe and it was empty. So was Jung's room.

ALEX: Wow.

JANET: Once in a while, I catch my dad looking out the
window. Most of the time he's looking for illegally
parked Japanese cars, but sometimes I think he's
looking for Jung.

ALEX: Where is he now?

JANET: I don't know. Heard he was in rehab for a while. He meets my mom at church sometimes.

Beat.

ALEX: Sorry to hear that.

JANET: That's okay.

Beat.

ALEX: That your camera bag?

JANET: Yup.

Beat.

ALEX: Are you a photographer?

JANET: Yup.

ALEX: How'd you become a photographer?

JANET: OCAD [Ontario College of Art and Design]. How'd you become a cop?

ALEX: Cop school. (*JANET chuckles.*) No, my life changed a lot after I moved out of this neighbourhood. I forgot how much you used to follow us around.

JANET: Can I take your picture?

ALEX: Uh, sure, okay.

JANET gets her camera. ALEX does a "hot cops" pose. JANET chuckles.

ALEX: Just playin'.

JANET: What did you have for breakfast?

ALEX: For breakfast?

JANET: Yeah.

ALEX: Cereal, some fruit, coffee.

JANET begins shooting.

JANET: What kind of cereal did you have?

ALEX: Mini-Wheats.

JANET: Have you always had Mini-Wheats?

ALEX: No, used to be Frosted Flakes — when I was a kid.
My dad liked Frosted Flakes. We'd eat it together.
We had this routine, this tiger thing we'd do.
"They're grrrreat!" Yeah, Frosted Flakes.

JANET: What about Cheerios?

ALEX: Nah.

JANET: What's wrong with Cheerios?

ALEX: For me, it had to do with what the cereal did to the milk. That bowlful of sweetened milk right at the end was what breakfast was all about.

JANET: Like the chocolate tip at the bottom of an ice cream Drumstick?

ALEX: Exactly.

Beat.

JANET: Wanna see?

ALEX: Sure. (*JANET shows ALEX his picture on the LCD screen.*) Wow. I look so . . . artsy. (*JANET giggles.*) What?

JANET: I was actually on my way to check out a site for a wedding I got tomorrow —

ALEX: When I came in?

JANET: When you came in.

ALEX: Where you shooting?

JANET: The Distillery. Where you shooting? That was a joke.

ALEX: Need a lift?

JANET: I gotta cover for my dad.

ALEX: Til when?

JANET: Another ten minutes? (*Beat.*) You married?

ALEX: Yeah, no — used to be. Divorced. You married?

JANET: No. Any kids?

ALEX: No. You?

JANET: No. But I want kids. Like, if I met the right guy
         and got married to him, then yeah, of course, no
         question, absolutely.

         JANET ducks down behind the counter.

ALEX: What kind of guy you looking for, maybe I can
         keep an eye out for you. (*Beat.*) Did you eat lunch?

JANET: No. You?

         *JANET rises with her hair undone, all sexy like,
         and proceeds to move in front of the counter.*

ALEX: No.

JANET: We could eat.

ALEX: We could. What do you want to eat?

JANET: I don't know. What do you want to eat?

ALEX: Anything's good.

JANET: Yeah, anything's good for me too.

ALEX: I'm not feeling anything in particular.

JANET: Me neither.

ALEX: Could do just about anything.

JANET: Yup, me too.

ALEX: You allergic to anything?

JANET: Melons.

ALEX: Melons? Really?

JANET: Yeah. Kinda developed it.

ALEX: Didn't know you could develop melons — allergies.

JANET: I used to not be allergic to melons, now I am.

ALEX: That's too bad. I love melons.

Beat.

JANET: Korean or Indian?

ALEX: Who?

JANET: Food. You. Choose. Korean or Indian?

ALEX: Korean.

JANET: Now it's your turn. Offer me a choice.

ALEX: Oh, okay, uh . . . Christie and Bloor . . . or Yonge and
Finch?

JANET: Christie and Bloor. Rice or noodles?

ALEX: Rice. Meat or vegetarian?

JANET: Meat. Pork or beef?

ALEX: Pork. Hot and spicy or extremely hot and spicy?

JANET: Extremely hot and spicy. In a stone bowl or in a
stainless steel bowl?

ALEX: Stone bowl. Gamjatang or pork mandu soondubu?

JANET: Gamja Tang. Kachi or Booungee?

ALEX: Han Kuk Kwan.

14. Take over the store

APPA: *Offstage. Returning from the back of the store, talking on the phone.* No, it's Christie —

ALEX: I'll pick you up in ten minutes.

ALEX exits. Bell. JANET returns behind the counter and begins to put on some makeup.

APPA: — then Bathurst, then Spadina, St. George, Bay, Yonge, Sherbourne, then is Castle Frank. Yah, one hundred percent guarantee. Yah, okay. (*APPA hangs up the phone.*) 아이씨 바보. [Idiot.] (*APPA pulls out JANET's Day-timer and reads from it.*) Okay, Janet, lesson number two: "Old is cold, new out of view." Old can is cold can, put in front. New can is not cold can, put out of view. "Old is cold, new out of view."

JANET: Appa, where'd you find that?

APPA: Upstair washroom.

JANET: I've been looking for that. Give it to me.

APPA: Wait, lesson number three is —

JANET: Appa, I gotta go.

APPA: Wait, we have to finish training, I make list —

JANET: Appa, I'm not taking over the store.

APPA: Janet, you is thirty years old now and still single. You have to understand, now is desperation time for you. Sudden death, overtime, penalty kick shootout. Expiration date is over. Take over store is only choice you having.

JANET: I can't believe —

APPA: Me and Umma is struggle whole life make life for you. We do what we have to do, hope you can be doctor, lawyer, big success, but what you do? Take picture. We don't have to come to Canada for you take picture. Even you can take picture in North Korea.

JANET: Appa —

APPA: Janet, I am dying . . . one day in future and before I dying, I —

JANET: You want to retire.

APPA: What is my story? Hm? What is story of me, Mr. Kim? My whole life is this store. Everybody know this store, they know me. This store is my story. And if I just sell store, then my story is over. Who is Mr. Kim? Nobody know that. You take over store, my story keep going.

JANET: But Appa, that's life. Whether you choose it or get thrown into it, you make it what it is. And if you're not happy with your life, I'm sorry, but you can't expect me to make your life — I don't know — meaningful.

APPA: But I give my life, my story for you.

JANET: But you're the parent. You're supposed to.

APPA: Why is that supposed to? I don't have to give to you my life. I could throw you away as baby. I don't have to love you as baby, but I do. That is choosing. I choose like that. So, you have to be thank you and give to me you life. Second half. Fifty-fifty. That's fair. Yah, lookit, I am work at store, what you do, you don't work at store and still you eat, sleep upstair, yah? You whole life, that's how we doing. Thirty years. So, just switch side now, like soccer. Second half, you work at store and I don't work at store and still I eat, sleep upstair. Understand? (*Beat.*) I'm not live more than ten years, it's good deal for you.

JANET: That's a messed-up idea, Appa.

APPA: What you talking?

JANET: That's a seriously messed-up idea.

APPA: YOU seriously messed up —

JANET: No, Appa, that's —

APPA: YOU no.

JANET: No, Appa, really —

APPA: YOU really.

JANET: Stop doing that!

APPA: YOU stop.

JANET: Give me my Day-timer, Appa!

APPA: Take out garbage and I give to you. (*JANET ties the garbage bag to take it out.*) What you doing? (*APPA unties what JANET has done and ties it his way.*) Have to roll like this. Push out air. Make tight. Small package. Then tie round back. That's best way.

    APPA offers it to JANET. JANET takes it and unties what APPA has done and reties it.

JANET: That's your way. And if it matters that much to you, then do it yourself.

APPA: Janet, that's you job.

JANET: My job? I haven't taken out the garbage in sixteen years. All of a sudden it's my job again? Fine. But it wasn't even my job back then, 'cuz if it were my job, then I would've gotten paid. So, what in fact I did back then and am doing right now is a favour for you. I wish you would at least appreciate this favour I'm doing for you, Appa.

JANET leaves with the garbage bag. Bell.

APPA: You pay rent? You pay for food? (*APPA follows JANET.*) What you talking? Take picture. Take picture! What's that?! Waste!!!

JANET returns with the garbage bag. Bell.

JANET: For my whole life, I've worked at least four hours a day covering for you guys, and I've never asked you for anything in return. I've never complained about it and never bitched about not getting paid. I've been here for you for my whole life, APPA. When Jung left, I was here. When Umma was sick, I was here. What would be nice is a simple thank-you. A little appreciation, that's all I need. To hear you say "thank you." Just once. (*APPA remains silent. JANET drops the garbage bag.*) Okay, fine. (*She goes behind the counter, takes out the printing calculator, and punches in the numbers.*) Four hours a day, six days a week, fifty-two weeks a year, for the past twenty years, eight dollars an hour — subtract room and board . . . You owe me a grand total of $102,720! Give me my money, Appa!

Beat.

APPA: Piano lesson. Piano lesson. $20 every lesson. Once a week. Every week. Five years. I pay.

JANET tallies it up.

APPA: Golf lesson. $500. I invest in you.

JANET tallies it up.

APPA: Summer art camp. Material fee. $200. Every year.

JANET tallies it up.

APPA: Winter church camp. $100. Blue Mountain ski pass —

JANET: Wait.

APPA: Blue Mountain ski pass. $50. Grade 8 semi-formal dress —

JANET: Wait.

APPA: Prom dress —

JANET: Wait!

APPA: Diet program. Dating program. Orthodontist. (*JANET stops tallying the numbers.*) Computer. Camera. Hand phone. Tuition fee. Trip to Korea. TTC Metropass. Weight-losing program. Internet. Shoes. Clothes. Haircut. Everything you have Appa give to you. All Appa having, Appa invest to you and what you doing? Waste time. Waste money. Waste hope. What I still owe to you? Tell to me, Janet. I give to you my whole life, what fucking I still owe to you!?

Beat.

JANET: My Day-timer.

APPA hurls the Day-timer at the front door.

APPA: Ahhhhhh!

JANET slowly gets the Day-timer and walks out. Bell.

Beat. Bell. UMMA returns.

UMMA: 아이고, 내 정신 좀 봐. 맨날 이래, 맨날. [Oh my goodness, look at me, always forgetting things, always.] (*UMMA takes an envelope from underneath the tray in the cash register. Beat.*) 왜 그래요? 뭔일 있어요? [What's wrong? What is it?]

APPA: 아니야. [Never mind.]

UMMA: 여보? 여보? [Honey? Honey?]

APPA exits to the back.

Kim's Convenience debuts at the 2011 Toronto Fringe Festival.

"Steal or no steal." Appa (Paul Sun-Hyung Lee) keeps his eye on a potential shoplifter. (This and all subsequent photos are from Soulpepper Theatre's 2012 production of *Kim's Convenience*.)

Michael Cooper

Above: Police officer Alex (Clé Bennett), a childhood friend of Jung, comes to the store to answer a 9-11 call.

Left: Actor Clé Bennett.

Michael Cooper

Appa suggests that Janet (Esther Jun) take over the store.

Umma (Jean Yoon) meets Jung (Ins Choi) at church.

Umma remembers naming her son, while Appa remembers naming the store.

Left: Jung returns to the store after a sixteen-year absence.

Below: Appa is startled when he sees Jung.

Michael Cooper

Michael Cooper

Above: Jung gives a photo of his son to Appa.

Right: Actor and play-wright Ins Choi.

Queen Street East and Seaton Street in Moss Park/Regent Park. It took us a very long time to locate the real store that would be our store. We then designed our store in the studio to match it. The owners allowed us to keep our signs up for the entire shoot and run of Season One. Off to the right is a bit of the commissioned mural by Toronto artist Elicser Elliot.

Vicky Peters

Early design renderings of the apartment above the store.
Art Director: James Oswald

Emilie Poulin

Early design renderings of the store.
Production Designer: John Dondertman

Paul Sun-Hyung Lee as Appa.

Three members of the Kim family: Umma, Appa, and Janet.

Episode: Photos at the Store
APPA: How much you think I get for this?

Jean Yoon as Umma.
Makeup: Geralyn Wraith

Andrea Bang as Janet.
Costume Design: Ruth Secord

Andrew Phung as Kimchee. Simu Liu as Jung.
Hair: Renee Chan

Episode: Gay Discount

UMMA *shuts the door, locks it.*
UMMA: It's family emergency.
JUNG: Is everyone okay?

Episode: Wingman

JANET: Appa, where's Umma?
APPA: Last time I see her she is in love shack with
Mr. Chin and two Russian hairstylist.

15. Hi Jung

UMMA sees the garbage bag and puts it in the closet.
UMMA begins to sing as she gets her things together
to leave.

UMMA: 천사의 말을 하는 사람도
사랑 없으면 소용이 없고
[If I speak in the language of heaven,
but speak it without love, it means nothing.]

JUNG enters with a knapsack on. He sings in harmony
with UMMA.

UMMA &
JUNG: 심오한 진리 깨달은 자도
울리는 징과 같네
[If I understand all mysteries,
but understand them without love,
it means nothing.]

하나님 말씀 전한다 해도
그 무슨 소용있나
사랑 없으면 소용이 없고
아무것도 아닙니다
[What meaning is there even in sharing
the message of God
if it is shared without love?
Anything, without love,
amounts to nothing.]
[*Based on 1 Corinthians 13:1–2*]

UMMA's church sanctuary at night.

UMMA: You remember church family singing contest? You was eight years old. Janet was six. We is stand up here in church. You, me, Appa, Janet, all together, hold hands. We win first place. That is my most happy memory.

JUNG: What about the time when I was born, Umma?

UMMA: That is my most painful memory. You work today?

JUNG: Yeah. What's with all the decorations?

UMMA: This Sunday is last day. Last day for our church.

JUNG: The condo thing? They bought it?

UMMA: Yah.

JUNG: 3.2?

UMMA: $3.9 million.

JUNG: Wow. Now you guys can move to North York. Buy a church with a parking lot.

UMMA: Our church is not moving.

JUNG: What, you guys gonna be at the bottom of the condo?

UMMA: They is closing our church.

JUNG: Who? The condo company?

UMMA: Church head office think waste of money to build
new church. Not enough people. So, they closing
our church and using money for mission work
in North Korea. Bible say time to start, time to
finish. Now is time to finish. When Moksanim
first start church, only six Korean church in
Toronto. All downtown, small, no money. Now,
over two hundred Korean church, all move out
of downtown, big building, lots of money. We is
last Korean downtown church.

Beat.

JUNG: Here, I got something for you.

JUNG gives UMMA a photo.

UMMA: Wah! Sonam. He is get so big. Two months?

JUNG: Yeah.

UMMA: Looks like six months old.

JUNG: Yeah, people say he's really big for his age.

UMMA: Looks just like Janet when she was baby.

UMMA offers the photo back.

JUNG: Keep it. It's yours.

UMMA: Appa should know he is *halabujee* now.

JUNG: How's Janet doing?

UMMA: She is still single, ready to mingle.

JUNG: Hey Umma, you ever think Janet might be "the gay"?

UMMA: The gay? If Janet is lesbian, that's okay because then at least I know reason why she has no boyfriend. *(UMMA gives JUNG the envelope.)* For baby.

JUNG: Thanks, Umma.

JUNG kisses UMMA on the cheek.

UMMA: What's wrong, Jung?

JUNG: I'm not happy.

UMMA: Can't always be happy, Jung.

JUNG: I don't like my life, Umma. I was at work today — do you know what Facebook is, Umma?

UMMA: Facebook?

JUNG: It's a website on the Internet. It's kinda like email, but it connects more people. And friends can find other friends and there's lots of photos — you remember Mike from church, long time ago, he was on the soccer team?

UMMA: 깍두기 아줌마 아들? [The son of that woman who makes that radish kimchee?]

JUNG: Yeah, right. He found me on Facebook today and soon the whole crew found me, the old church soccer team. We're all chatting away, checking out photos, like a reunion. Suyoung put up an old picture of the team, and he starts writing this play-by-play. Centennial Park, Etobicoke. The Toronto Korean inter-church annual soccer tournament. Under-16 division. Game one, Haninjangno Church: (*explosion sound*) conquered. Game two, Dong Bu Church: (*explosion sound*) conquered. Game three, Bethel Church: tied. Quarter-finals, United church: (*explosion sound*). Semi-finals, Young Nak Church: (*explosion sound*). Final championship game, the Catholic church: tied. Extra time: tied. Extra extra time: tied. Penalty kick shootout: (UMMA *joins in on making the explosion sound*). So glorious, right? Mike lives in Richmond Hill. He drives a Beemer. 5 series. He's got great-looking kids, a sexy cute wife, family vacations all around the world every year. I've seen all his photos. Jason, Rich, Tech, Tom, Henry, Mike, Jong, Young, Young Jong, Suyoung. All of them. They're all successful. They start asking about me. What I do, where I been. I start making stuff up, trying desperately hard to sound impressive, but just sounding desperate. I was their captain. I was their captain, Umma. I was smarter than all of them, faster, stronger. I didn't dream I'd end up renting cars to people. Nine to five. Checking for dents and scratches. Living in a shithole in Parkdale. Apartment's a constant mess. Fight all the time, his mom and me. She thinks I'm a loser — I don't even know why I'm with her anymore. And all he ever does is cry and cry and cry and cry and cry. Just wanna leave, y'know? Just go. Start over. Somewhere else. Calgary, Vancouver — doesn't matter where. It'd be so easy too. Bay and Dundas, hop on a bus and leave. I rent cars to people, then take the street-car home. What is that? That's a joke.

Beat.

UMMA: You Appa was teacher in Korea. He was very good teacher. Student all love him. He have lots of friend. We have very good life in Korea. Then we coming to Canada. But he can't be teacher here. His English is very . . . no good. We get store. And he work every day. No weekend, no time off, no vacation, always have to be open, no retirement. Why? Why he doing like that? For you. For you and Janet. He is choosing

like that for you. (*Offers the photo.*) You choosing
like that for him. (*JUNG takes the photo.*)

JUNG: How's Appa doing, anyway?

UMMA: Appa is getting old. You remember Mr. Lee?

JUNG: Black man with the Korean last name?

UMMA: Yah. He is make offer to buy store.

JUNG: Appa selling the store?

UMMA: No, Mr. Lee just make offer.

JUNG: How much?

UMMA: Enough to retire.

JUNG: What's Appa gonna do?

UMMA: I don't know. Go home, Jung. Go home.

JUNG exits.

16. Naming

A memory of APPA *and* UMMA. *Underscored.*

APPA: What you think, Kim's Variety Store?

UMMA: Kim's Variety Store?

APPA: Yah. Kim's Variety Store. What you think?

UMMA: Mr. Kim has already.

APPA: Who Mr. Kim?

UMMA: Yonge and Finch Mr. Kim.

APPA: Mr. Kim, Yonge and Finch, has Kim's Variety Store? Then just Kim's Variety. Take out "store." What you think?

UMMA: Kim's Variety?

APPA: Yah.

UMMA: St. George Mr. Kim has already.

APPA: St. who?

UMMA: St. George.

APPA: Who is St. George?

UMMA: St. George is St. George.

APPA: St. George? Sound like St. Jajee.

UMMA: Not St. Jajee, St. George.

APPA: Kim Cheese. Like Mac's Milk, but Kim and cheese.

UMMA: We don't only sell cheese.

APPA: Mac's don't only sell milk. (*Beat.*) 7-Twelve. Like
         7-Eleven but . . . (*Beat.*) KFC. Kim's First Convenience.
         No, people think we is Kentucky Fries Chicken.
         Then we have to sell chicken, fries, and turkey.
         (*Beat.*) Kim Hortons.

UMMA: *Rubbing her belly.* What you think of name is Jung?
         (*Pause.*) If baby is boy, Jung Kim. What you think?

17. What is it?

Store. Night.

APPA: 언제 왔어? [When did you get in?]

UMMA: 조금 전에요. 내가 해논거 다 먹었어요? [Just got
         here. Did you eat?]

APPA: 먹었어. 왜 그래? [Yeah. What is it?]

UMMA: 아니에요 ... Janet 은 요? [Nothing ... Where's Janet?]

APPA: 나갔겠지. 주일날 최집사님이 저녁 같이 하자네. 듣고있어? 왜 그러냐니까? [Out. Mr. Chae wants to have us over for dinner this Sunday. Did you hear me? What's wrong?]

UMMA: 아니에요. 당신이 알아서 해요. 저 먼저 올라가요. [Nothing. Yeah, it's fine. I'm going up.]

APPA: 뭐냐니까? 여보? 여보? 여보? 아이씨 참! [What is it? Honey? Honey?]

UMMA takes the tray of food and exits to the back.

APPA looks at Mr. Lee's offer and picks up the phone.

18. Who you go out with?

JANET enters. Bell.

JANET: Closing?

APPA: Soon.

JANET: Want some help?

APPA: It's okay.

JANET: How's business?

APPA: Same same. (*JANET begins to exit to the back.*)
You go out?

JANET: Yeah.

APPA: Who you go out with?

JANET: Alex.

APPA: Alex? Black police Alex?

JANET: *Coming forward.* Yes.

APPA: You used to have crush on him. You have fun time?

JANET: Yeah.

APPA: *Beat.* You remember Mr. Chae?

JANET: Ingoo's Appa?

APPA: Yah. He is having store in South Central L.A.,
California. Lots of black people is living there too.
One day black lady is come and ask five-dollar loan.
So, he give loan five dollar. Next week, she come and
pay back. No interest. Then she ask loan ten dollar.
And he give and she pay back. And continue. They

have good friendship. She tell all her friend, and they come and ask loan too. He is help all of them. Then 1992. Rodney King L.A. riot happen. All Korean convenience store is on fire and black people stealing. So he take shotgun and go to store. When he gets out of car, he see fire and smoke, people screaming, running, crazy, and he look at store. He see all black people in front of store. So, he get gun, ready to shoot, then he stop. What he see is that black woman who he give to loan and all his black customer hold hand, make big wall, stop other people stealing his store.

Beat.

JANET: What are you trying to say, Appa?

APPA: Alex is not Korean, but if you want to marry him, that's okay with me.

JANET: We went out on one date. I don't even know if he had a good time.

19. Let's talk

Bell.

ALEX: Hi.

APPA: Alex.

ALEX: *To JANET.* Can I talk to you?

APPA: Yah, okay, talk.

ALEX: Uh, I didn't —

APPA: No, it's okay.

ALEX: No, Mr. Kim, I didn't mean —

APPA: Alex, it's okay, take easy, nice and slow. We is here
        for you. Talk. (*Beat.*) We closing soon. Hurry up.

ALEX: Uh, okay. I have this, uh, friend, this girl, who's just
        a friend.

APPA: Okay.

ALEX: She recently met an old friend of hers, uh, this guy.

APPA: Okay.

ALEX: They used to know each other when they were kids.
        I mean, he was best friends with her brother and she'd
        always be around and he never thought much of her,
        growing up — see, the thing is, he was a bad kid.

APPA: Oh.

ALEX: And she knows all about the stuff he used to do, like
        really stupid stuff. Anyway, so they meet and they

go out . . . on this date, I guess, and, well, it wasn't like an official date per se, but . . . uh . . . Sorry, this was a bad idea. (*Makes to leave.*)

APPA: Alex! Do you think she like him?

ALEX: Who?

APPA: You friend.

ALEX: Oh, uh, I don't know. I'm not sure.

APPA: Janet, do you think she like him?

JANET: Uh —

APPA: Okay, Alex, do you think he like her?

ALEX: Um, that's a good question, Mr. Kim. Well, uh, see, ever since his divorce . . . uh . . . see, the thing about it is, he went through this phase where —

APPA: Okay, that's enough! Alex, do you believing in the Jesus?

ALEX: What?

JANET sighs.

APPA: Do you believing in the Jesus?

ALEX: Yes, I believing in the Jesus.

APPA: You have job?

JANET: Appa —

ALEX: I'm a cop.

APPA: Do you think my Janet is the sexy?

JANET: Appa!

ALEX: What?

APPA: Do you think my Janet is the sexy?

JANET: Appa!

ALEX: Mr. Kim — AH!

         APPA twists ALEX's hand, forcing ALEX to his knees, writhing in pain.

JANET: Appa! What the hell are you doing?

APPA: You want to know answer? Alex, do you think my Janet is the sexy? Yes or no?

ALEX: Yes!

         APPA lets him go.

APPA: Good. (*Beat.*) Then give to her popo.

JANET: Appa, stop it!

ALEX: What? You want me to give her a popo?

APPA: Yah.

ALEX: What's a popo? (*APPA kisses the air twice.*) You want me to kiss your daughter?

APPA: Yah.

ALEX: Now?

APPA: Yah.

ALEX: In front of you?

APPA: My store, my business.

> ALEX *slowly, awkwardly kisses* JANET. *Then she kisses him. Then he goes in for another kiss and* APPA *grabs his arm in such a way that* ALEX *is up on his toes, writhing in pain.*

APPA: What's you problem, Alex?

ALEX: What? You told me to give her a popo.

APPA: Do I tell you popo two times?

ALEX: She popo me.

APPA: I know she popo you, I see she is popo you, I was here, I was supervise. But then you try popo her one more time after she popo you. Two popo, too many popo.

ALEX: Sorry.

APPA lets him go.

APPA: Okay. Now, step two. Do step two.

Beat.

ALEX: You're gonna have to give me some clarification on what step two is, Mr. Kim.

APPA: 아이씨 참! [Good grief!] Step two is, ask Janet marry you.

ALEX &
JANET: What?

APPA: Ask Janet marry you.

ALEX: Mr. Kim — (*APPA twists ALEX's hand, forcing ALEX to his knees, writhing in pain.*) Ah!

JANET: Appa, just stop — (*JANET tries to pull APPA's hand off ALEX. APPA then twists JANET's hand, forcing her to her knees, writhing in pain.*) Ah!

APPA *has both of them on either side of him, on their knees, writhing in pain.*

APPA: Alex, do step two.

ALEX: Mr. Kim —

JANET: Appa —

APPA: Alex, do step two.

ALEX: Ah! Janet, will you marry me?

JANET: Ah! Appa, this is ridiculous!

APPA: Ask again!

ALEX: Janet, will you marry me?

APPA: Janet, say yes.

JANET: Stop! Ow!

APPA: Ask again!

ALEX: (*simultaneously*) Ah! Janet will you marry me!? Ahhhhh!

JANET: (*simultaneously*) Ah! Appa, you're ruining everything!

APPA: (*simultaneously*) Janet, say yes! This is last chance for you — AH! (*ALEX does a reversal and has APPA in a hold.*)

ALEX: I'm sorry, Mr. Kim. I'm sorry. I just need to talk — I came here to talk to your daughter.

APPA: Okay, hurry up, talk.

ALEX: Uh, okay. Um. Janet, I've always thought of you as a younger sister, following us around like a chubby little puppy dog. Wait, but when I saw you today, like, now — you're so beautiful. You're smart, talented, you make me laugh — I don't understand why you're still single. The only way I can figure it is God must love me so much that he's kept you single for all these years to bless me with you.

JANET: I've had a crush on you since I was ten years old, Alex. Still do.

ALEX: Seriously?

JANET: Seriously.

ALEX: I'm off tomorrow, you wanna do something?

JANET: I got a wedding to shoot.

ALEX: Need a helper?

JANET: You wanna be my assistant?

ALEX: I do.

JANET: Pick me up at seven a.m.?

ALEX: I'll be here.

> ALEX *and* JANET *go in for a kiss, inadvertently putting pressure on* APPA's *hand.*

APPA: AH!

JANET: What about him?

ALEX: Come here. Apply pressure right here.

> *They transfer holding* APPA.

APPA: AH!

ALEX: Bye, Janet.

JANET: Bye.

ALEX: Please don't hold this against me, Mr. Kim. I just needed to talk to your daughter.

APPA: Okay, see you.

> ALEX *exits. Bell.*

APPA: Okay, Janet, enough is enough, let go.

JANET: Thank you.

APPA: You welcome. Now let go.

JANET: "Thank you . . . Janet." (*Beat.*) Repeat. After. Me.

APPA: What? Ah!

JANET: Repeat after me. "Thank you, Janet."

APPA: AH!

JANET: Repeat after me. "Thank you —"

APPA: You welcome.

JANET: Repeat after me! "Thank you, Janet!"

APPA: Ah! Ah! Okay, okay, okay. Thank you, Janet. Okay, enough is enough, let go.

JANET: "I'm sorry."

APPA: That's okay. Ah!

JANET: Repeat after me. "I'm sorry."

APPA: Ah! Okay, okay, I'm sorry.

JANET: "I love you, Janet. I love you, Janet." (*Beat.*) "I love you, Janet!"

APPA: Ah! Okay! I love you, Janet!

JANET releases APPA.

JANET: I love you too, Appa. (*With arms open.*) And see, no one's twisting my arm to say it.

JANET slowly lowers her arms, picks up her bag, and walks to the back of the store.

APPA: You was fourteen years old. (*JANET stops.*) You was fourteen years old, school project: "What I am most proud of." You write story how we begin store. Then you take picture of me in front of store. That is my most happy memory, Janet. I don't want you take over store. I want you live life best way you choosing.

JANET takes the garbage bag from the closet and approaches the front door.

APPA: Yah. (*APPA takes it from her.*) Go upstair. Go. Sleep. (*JANET embraces APPA.*) Okay, okay, okay, that's good enough, let go, Janet.

JANET exits to the back and APPA takes the garbage out. Bell. APPA returns. Bell. Turns off the lights. Goes to the cash register.

20. Hi Appa

Bell. JUNG *enters with a knapsack on, no tie, and shirt dishevelled.*

APPA: Sorry, we is closing.

JUNG: Hi, Appa. (*Beat.*) How you been? (*Beat.*) You look good. I take it the store's doing well? (*Beat.*) Still smells the same. A good smell. Familiar.

APPA: You voice is change.

JUNG: Sorry?

APPA: You voice, you voice is . . . change.

JUNG: My voice. Right. Yeah, I guess it has. Your English got a lot better.

APPA: Umma is upstair. I go call her.

APPA *makes to leave.*

JUNG: That's, uh — that's alright. Um . . . (*Beat.*) What is that? What are those? Energy drinks? Insam Energy drinks?

APPA: Yah. New one. From Korea.

JUNG: KBA?

APPA: Mr. Park bring in. (*Beat. Offers one.*) You can have.

JUNG: That's okay. (*As APPA is about to put the can back.*) Sure, yeah, okay.

JUNG walks to the counter and takes the can from APPA. He cracks it open and takes a sip.

APPA: What you think?

JUNG: It's good. Yeah, it's really good. Not too sweet. Not too mediciny. (*Seeing the price.*) A dollar fifty? You could sell this for two dollars to black people and two-fifty to white people. Rock Star, Red Bull, they go for, like, three in my neighbourhood.

APPA: Oh, yah?

JUNG: Yeah.

APPA: That's kind of rip-off.

JUNG: Yeah, it is. I was just . . . How's Janet?

APPA: Good.

JUNG: Still single, ready to mingle?

APPA: She has boyfriend now.

JUNG: She has a boyfriend now?

APPA: Yah.

JUNG: You sure?

APPA: Yah, I was supervise. (*Beat.*) She is upstair too.

JUNG: Lotta condos going up, eh? It'll be good for business. A good location is finally building itself around the store. (*Beat.*) Remember when I wanted to run the store all by myself? I was eleven. You told me I was too short, so I went to the back of the store, strapped milk crates onto my feet, and came out walking tall. (*Steps up on a milk crate, then steps down.*) You were so impressed you let me run it for twenty minutes, all by myself. Eight customers.

APPA: I let you run store all by you self because you pass my test.

JUNG: Right. Your Korean history test.

APPA: My proud moment Korea history test.

JUNG: Right.

APPA: *Beat.* 1592. 1592.

JUNG: 1592? Oh, uh, that's Admiral Yi-Soon Shin invents the Turtle Ship. The world's first ironclad battleship in 1592.

APPA: Sixty-six.

JUNG: 1966 World Cup soccer. North Korea beats Italy in the sixteens to advance to the quarter-finals.

APPA: Eighty-four.

JUNG: 1984. Hyundai's Pony arrives in Canada in 1984. Its initial 5,000-unit projection totals at 50,000 units sold, becoming Canada's best-selling car that year.

APPA: Sea of Japan.

JUNG: Sea of Japan doesn't exist. The body of water between Korea and Japan is called the East Sea.

APPA: Kim Hyung-Soon.

JUNG: Kim Hyung-Soon. The Korean guy in America who crossed a peach and a plum, inventing the nectarine.

APPA: Ninety-eight.

JUNG: Ninety-eight? 1998. Uh . . . LPGA. Se Ri Pak becomes the first non-White woman to ever win the LPGA golf championship, which is still dominated by Korean women today.

APPA: O-two.

JUNG: 2002 World Cup soccer, hosted by South Korea and Japan. Korea placed fourth. Also, 2002 international breakdance champion is a Korean guy named Bruce

Lee. He did this one move, Appa, oh, you gotta
YouTube him.

APPA: Ten.

JUNG: 2010. Vancouver Olympics. Yuna Kim wins the gold
medal in figure skating, beating out that Japanese
girl.

APPA: Thirteen.

JUNG: Thirteen? Uh . . . Park Ji-Sung. His number. The
captain of South Korea's national soccer team. And
Manchester United's midfielder. Third Lung. They
call him Third Lung 'cuz he's not a finesse player,
but he never gives up.

APPA: Good. Very good.

JUNG: I have a son, Appa. He's two months old. That's right,
you're a *halabujee* now. (*Gives him the photo.*) That's
him. He's really big for his age. I was thinking maybe
if I start him early enough, he could make the NHL.
First Korean NHL superstar. What do you think?

APPA: What his name?

JUNG: Sonam. Sonam Kim. It's a Tibetan name. It means
"The Fortunate One."

APPA: His mommy is Korean?

JUNG: No. She's Tibetan. She's from Tibet.

APPA: You married?

JUNG: Yeah. No. No, I'm not married.

APPA: What you doing job? Working?

JUNG: Yeah, I rent cars to people. I work at Discount Car Rental in Parkdale.

APPA: You like working at Discount?

JUNG: I hate it. I can't stand working there. It's just, with my record, it's . . . um . . .

        Beat.

APPA: I think of you, Jung. I think of you lots of time. Every day. You was very smart kid. Good looking. Natural leader. Lots of girl like you. Good at sports, music, lots of thing. You was so full of . . .

JUNG: Potential.

APPA: Yah, potential. Could be best, I always dream like that. Could be best. But that is my dream, not you dream. (*Beat.*) If Sonam don't become NHL super-star, don't get angry, it's okay. You can still be proud of him. You understand?

JUNG: Can I work here, Appa? What do you think of me working here? I could stock, clean, y'know, go to KBA, do the wholesale pickup, research all the best prices in town. You wouldn't have to pay me that much and you could always cash out. I don't have to handle the money. What do you say?

APPA: Take over store.

JUNG: What?

APPA: Take over store, Jung.

JUNG: What? You want me to take over the store?

APPA: Yah.

JUNG: You giving the store to me?

APPA: Yah.

JUNG: Seriously?

APPA: Seriously.

JUNG: No, Appa, seriously?

APPA turns to JUNG with tears streaking down his face.

APPA: This is my serious face.

JUNG: Store's probably worth a lot of money. You could sell it and retire. Why do you want to give it to me?

APPA: What is my story? What is story of Mr. Kim? My whole life I doing store. This store is my story? No. My story is not Kim's Convenience. My story is you. And Janet. And Umma. And Sonam. You understand? (*JUNG nods his head yes.* APPA *gets the pricing gun and offers it to* JUNG.) Change price. Make two dollar. That's good idea. (*JUNG takes the pricing gun with both of his hands.*)

APPA *exits to the back.*

JUNG *goes behind the counter, adjusts the numbers on the pricing gun, and begins repricing the cans.*

Lights slowly fade to the sound of the pricing gun.

REFLECTIONS ON
KIM'S CONVENIENCE
From Stage to Screen

ALBERT SCHULTZ
Founding Artistic Director of Soulpepper Theatre
Executive Producer of *Kim's Convenience*, the TV Series

I am sitting behind a set at a studio in downtown Toronto, watching a scene take shape on a monitor behind the set of *Kim's Convenience*, the television series. On the other side of the wall is a creative army of actors, technicians, and craftspeople.

Sitting on my right are two men, Ins Choi and Ivan Fecan, one who was once my student and one who was once my boss, and both of whom have become valued friends and collaborators. Now all three of us are wearing audio headsets, sitting in classic canvas folding chairs with the words "Executive Producer" emblazoned on the back.

Pinch me.

So many people wanted to help Soulpepper bring *Kim's Convenience* to the small screen. The play's mixture of funny and heartwarming make it a perfect fit for television, and the fact that it speaks so eloquently to the first-generation experience makes it such an emblematic story for twenty-first-century Canada. We always felt that the CBC was where this show belonged, but we needed the perfect partner to help us get it there.

I met Ivan Fecan many years ago when I was a young actor with a big break at the CBC, where Ivan was in charge. He had approved me to be the new addition to the already well-established cast of *Street Legal*, the network's leading series. Before he went off to build CTV into a national network, Ivan supported me in many ventures at the CBC. About a decade ago, when Ivan was still with CTV, we worked on another project together and it was at this time that Ivan and his wife, Sandra Faire, became involved philanthropically with Soulpepper. I had always admired Ivan and knew him to be tremendously smart and passionately Canadian.

One fateful day I invited Ivan to witness the first run-through of Weyni Mengesha's beautiful production of *Kim's Convenience*. From that moment on he has been the show's biggest supporter and, with his great team at Thunderbird, Ivan has been instrumental in realizing Soulpepper's ambition and Ins Choi's dream.

I like to imagine Ins watching the first episode of this series with his parents and his children. I imagine the pride of his parents, who brought him to this country when he was a year old and who will be watching their son's stories told to a country full of people just like them . . . people who took extraordinary risks in coming to Canada . . . people who worked remarkably hard to build a life for their family and, in doing so, built a nation.

The series that we have made is about a country whose strength and vitality is derived from its diversity. I do not believe there has ever been a major television series *anywhere* with a more diverse cast than this one. I hope that for Ins's children, this is what television will look like for the rest of their lives.

IVAN FECAN
Executive Chair of Thunderbird Films
Executive Producer and Producer of *Kim's Convenience*, the TV Series

The journey from stage to screen began in December 2011, when Albert Schultz invited me to a rehearsal of the play *Kim's Convenience*. As usual, Albert had his reasons.

I first met Albert when he joined the cast of *Street Legal*. In addition to being mesmerizing in his role on screen, Albert also created the Matt Helm Boom Boom Room in his dressing room. Part speakeasy, part salon, complete with martinis, cigars, and God only knows what else, it flouted every CBC rule imaginable in the very sterile new CBC headquarters on Front Street in Toronto. Naturally, it became the destination of choice for every writer, director, actor, and musician there. Of course I have to say I didn't go, because as Vice President of CBC Television, I was supposed to enforce the rules.

Albert went on to be the founding artistic director of Soulpepper Theatre, which is a company of artists known for championing up-and-coming Canadian stage talent. We reconnected when he was doing a capital campaign for Soulpepper's gorgeous theatre complex in Toronto's Distillery District. As my wife, Sandra, and I can attest, Albert is also one hell of a fundraiser. Thus, our eponymous atrium.

Albert knew that *Kim's Convenience* had TV and film written all over it, but he wanted guidance. That's where I came in. I had just sold CTVglobemedia and was on my way to Santa Barbara for the winter. The play was due to premiere in January, so Albert asked whether I could attend a rehearsal just before Christmas.

The play blew me away. I am a child of refugees and *Kim's* is the universal Canadian immigrant story. It was so right for the times then and perhaps even more so today, with the influx of thousands of Syrian refugees.

After the rehearsal, Albert introduced me to Ins Choi, who, based on his experiences, created the play. The three of us went to lunch, where I gave them some advice. Ins was painfully shy and barely spoke a word. In honour of this being his inaugural showbiz lunch, he ordered his first ever Cobb salad, which of course was created at the Brown Derby in Hollywood. This was my first inkling that Ins was going to adapt very well to showbiz!

Cut to two years later. I had joined Thunderbird Film as Executive Chair. One of my first calls was to Albert to inquire what he had done with the rights to *Kim's*. To my delight, they were still available.

Thunderbird and Soulpepper immediately signed a development deal and *Kim's Convenience* became our first co-production. The next step was to recruit a showrunner to work with Ins, who very much wanted to stay with his creative baby. From my old CTV days, I immediately thought of Kevin White, the showrunner on the final two seasons of *Corner Gas*. It turns out that Kevin had seen the play and loved it. We organized a chemistry meeting and they both felt that they could work together. In fact, they have turned out to be a wonderful team. There was strong interest from every Canadian television network, but the CBC felt like the right home for this show, so we were delighted when they came on board.

As I write this from our studio not far from Regent Park, where the show is set, we are one month into production. With the CBC, various federal and provincial funding agencies, and Thunderbird, *Kim's* is fully financed in Canada. This is meaningful because with foreign money comes foreign input on scripts. Given how differently immigration is currently viewed in much of Europe and the U.S., it is important to provide a Canadian perspective on this subject, while telling the stories of the Kim family.

You will notice that, compared to the play, new characters are introduced and even existing characters altered slightly. We also meet the Kim family a few years earlier in their history. But the heart and soul of the universal story of immigrant parents doing their all to give their kids a better life is still very much there.

KEVIN WHITE
Co-Creator, Executive Producer,
Writer of *Kim's Convenience*, the TV Series

A number of years ago, my wife and I went to see *Kim's Convenience* at Soulpepper Theatre. We thought it was terrific. I laughed a lot and was even brought to tears, but more importantly I loved the voice behind the writing. I knew nothing of Ins and was surprised and delighted to discover he was also playing Jung at the time.

Skip ahead three years and I get a call from my agent, asking if I know anything about *Kim's Convenience*. He told me they were adapting it for television and that the playwright was looking to meet with writers. I told him I definitely wanted to take the meeting. Ins and I met for coffee and discussed the play, what I thought of the characters, and how it might be adapted for TV. I thought the meeting had gone well, but it was weeks before I heard anything back. Finally, I was told by my agent that Ins wanted to meet again. That seemed like a good sign until Ins told me that the reason he wanted to meet was because he'd kind of forgotten what we talked about the first time. I joked that I'd obviously left a deep impression. Nonetheless, we had a great second meeting and I came on board in the summer of 2014. Ins and I would meet in an empty classroom at Soulpepper, talking about the play and the characters and, of course, we wondered where the TV series should start. Should they start at the same point? Should the play effectively be the pilot? If so, what would it be like to see Jung at the store and the family reunited?

After some consideration, we weren't sure that was the best way to go. Part of what makes the play so strong is the conflict and unresolved nature of Appa and Jung's relationship.

We decided it might be better for the TV series to explore how the Kim family got to where they are in the play. As such, we rolled the clock back and imagined the family ten years younger than they are on stage. We wanted to see the characters grow and hoped they would have a long life. We wanted to see Janet begin studying photography. We wanted to see Jung starting his job at the car rental agency. We wanted to see Appa and Umma working at the store, day to day.

So for the series, Appa and Umma are in their mid-to-late fifties. It's 2016, and they continue to run the store they bought in 1984 at Sherbourne and Queen, sandwiched between the changing downtown neighbourhoods of Moss Park and Regent Park. Janet is twenty and studying photography at OCADU, and Jung is twenty-five and has just started working at Handy Car Rental.

We also meet Janet's friends at OCADU, Gerald and Semira. We meet Jung's best friend, co-worker, and roommate, "Kimchee" Han, who, like Jung, was a delinquent teenager. We also meet Shannon, their twenty-six-year-old boss from Cape Breton, who sometimes has trouble hiding the fact that she has eyes for Jung.

We also introduce Umma's circle of peers at church, including the well-heeled Mrs. Park, as well as Umma's more relaxed friend, Mrs. Lee. Finally, at the store we find Appa's friends dropping by, including Mr. Chin and Mr. Mehta, local Chinese and Indian business owners respectively, who together with Appa share a similar path to Canada from their homelands.

As we expanded the world around the store, story ideas started to come from this new mix of characters. What if Appa commissioned Janet's friend from school to take pictures of him instead of asking Janet? What if Jung was trying for a promotion at work? Would Umma be happy about it? Would his best friend be upset? The Kims' world expanded further as we brought on more writers, who offered their own ideas on the characters. What if Appa's widower friend Mr. Chin asked Appa to be his wingman on a date? What if Appa disciplined a kid at the store who happened to be the five-year-old son of Janet's photography professor?

These are just some of the premises that make up our first season. But they all grew from the beloved characters of the play. We just tried to colour in details of their lives that went beyond the boundaries of the stage.

While this may sound relatively straightforward, it was not. It took two years and tons of discussion, and there were plenty of creative missteps along the way. Early on, for example, Mr. Chin was Appa's nemesis, but we found it was better (and funnier) to have them as friends. Also, Janet's friend from school, Gerald, was originally conceived as a heavily pierced Goth. But when we cast the role, Ben Beauchemin brought a completely different vibe to the part and we loved it.

Another big shift was making Umma and Appa more contemporary. In the play the characters are modelled more on the generation of Koreans who came to Canada in the late '60s and early '70s. But in the series, they're more modern. They came to Canada in the '80s, when they were in their twenties. So Umma and Appa are more youthful in the TV version. They are still actively working, they have friends, they socialize, and Umma in particular is more mischievous and playful than what we saw on stage.

Hopefully these changes will further colour the already rich canvas Ins painted in the play. For me it's been both extremely fulfilling and daunting. You don't want to mess with a world that's so well drawn to begin with. Thankfully, the best part of the process has been Ins' generosity and friendship. It's not easy bringing on people to adjust and change your work, let alone a white guy with little exposure to Korean culture. But over the past two years, Ins and I have shared many family stories. We've had long chats with friends about their lives growing up in convenience stores, dry cleaners, and donut shops. We've shared *ssam gyup sal* and *galbi* and have probably laughed more than in any collaboration I can remember. That alone has made this project one of the most rewarding of my career.

JEAN YOON
Actor, Playing the Role of "Umma" in *Kim's Convenience*, the TV Series

All together, hold hands.

The refrain of the hymn Umma sings translates back from the Korean into English with unsettling directness: "Without love, there is no meaning... Without love, there is nothing at all." Every misguided squabble Appa picks with Janet, every day the Kims labour at the store, every disappointed aspiration for something better for their children is rooted in love. Umma reminds us of the cost of their life in Canada: "No weekend, no vacation, no time off, no retirement... Why? For you? He choose that way for *you*..." The play acknowledges the devotion and suffering of our parents' experience and offers the experience back to us as comedy with redemption and forgiveness. We witness Appa, through sheer force of love, surrender his pride and his anger to embrace his real dream, the only dream worth having — the love and integrity of his family, his wife and children, and his grandchildren — whatever path they choose.

I am deeply grateful to Ins Choi for writing this play, for his talent, for his devastatingly precise comedic observation, for his compassionate vision. I am grateful he asked me on board for Fringe show, grateful the show went on to grow through Soulpepper Theatre's support, grateful our story is now a television comedy series.

The story keeps on going…

As an actor, the television series offers me an opportunity to explore Umma when she is younger, more hopeful, still undeterred from her plan to marry off her children to good Christian-Korean partners with post-doctorate degrees. She's not yet defeated, not yet touched by regret. This Umma is as vigorous and comically out of step with her children's values as her husband. She goes on adventures of her own and has tender, nuanced, and rich relationships with family and friends. I spent all yesterday learning the B-52s song "Love Shack" and the Sonny and Cher classic "I Got You Babe" in preparation for upcoming scenes. Need I say more?

And every day I am on set, I think again of my own family, my beautiful mother and my kind and stoic father; the kind and quirky *ajimas* I have met on my travels; my grandparents — and I reach deep into all that love, all that family history, to make art.

How blessed am I.

You, me, Appa, Janet. All together. Hold hands.

PAUL SUN-HYUNG LEE
Actor, Playing the Role of "Appa" in *Kim's Convenience*, the TV Series

Gratitude. Of all words that I could use to describe my experiences with *Kim's Convenience*, "gratitude" is the one word that keeps springing to mind. As I write this, we're almost at the halfway point of shooting episodes for Season One of the television series and I am living in a dream. I wake up every morning excited about the day ahead and what new adventures the Kim family will embark on, and I return home exhausted and overjoyed by the work we've done. In many ways it's hard to believe we've come this far — from when I first got involved, reading a couple of scenes for the Toronto Diaspora Dialogues back in 2005; the numerous workshops over the next five years; premiering at the Toronto Fringe Festival in 2011; opening Soulpepper Theatre's 2012 season; embarking on a Canadian national tour from 2013 to 2015 to the cities of London, Port Hope, Calgary, Hamilton, Ottawa, Winnipeg, Vancouver, Edmonton, and five Toronto productions; and now filming the series produced by Thunderbird Film, Soulpepper Theatre, and airing on CBC.

I'm grateful to my wife, Anna, and my sons, Noah and Miles, for supporting me as I followed my dreams of performing this wonderful play across Canada on main stages of theatres I never thought I'd ever get the chance of playing on because of the colour of my skin. And while *Kim's Convenience* took their husband and dad away for weeks at a time, I'm grateful that on special occasions my family was able to join me and now they can say they've seen much of Canada from coast to coast.

I'm grateful my parents are still alive to see me perform what is essentially their story, and mine, in front of thousands of people across our adopted country.

I'm grateful my agent, Colleen, didn't blink an eye when I told her I *needed* to do *Kim's Convenience* for the Fringe, even though it meant not auditioning for paying gigs over a busy summer.

I'm grateful for my fellow cast mates over the life of *Kim's Convenience*: the Janets: Esther, Grace, and Chantelle; the Alexes: Clé and André; the Ummas: Jean and Jane; the Jungs: Ins, Dale, and Patrick; and to my new TV family: Andrea, Simu, Andrew, Nicole, and John. All professionals, all at the top of their game, and all beautiful, generous, and lovely human beings.

We are family. Now and forever.

I'm grateful for my touring family: Kat, Neha, A. J., Nancy, Weyni, Mike, Andrew, Lorenzo, and Ken.

I'm grateful for my Soulpepper family: Albert, Leslie, Claire, Laura, Fiona, Lisa, Molly, Farwah, Katie, and everyone upstairs and down.

I'm grateful to my new Thunderbird family: Ivan, Alex, Sandra, Robin, Nicola, Tim, et al.

I'm grateful to the CBC for picking up the show and for their wonderful support.

I'm grateful to Ins Choi for creating a world that is so authentic, so real, so recognizable that it echoes my own life in a way that I never, ever thought would be told on stage or on screen, and for letting me play a character so rich in life and love and allowing me to make his voice my own.

Gratitude.

And love.

So much love.

I hope you loved reading this play as much as I have loved performing it over the years. Many thanks.

Okseeyou.

INS CHOI
Co-Creator, Executive Producer, Writer of *Kim's Convenience*, the TV Series

I had never written for TV. I didn't even have screenwriting software. So, the first step was to find me a co-creator. Thunderbird and Soulpepper made a shortlist of names and I met with them all. One of them was Kevin White. I remember saying to my wife after that interview, "I dunno, he's so white. His name is even White." Be that as it may, he was a funny, smart, regular kinda guy, with a lot of writing and creating experience. He was a leader. He was a good listener. He was perceptive. He spoke French. So began the process of Kevin and I expanding the world of the play to fit and fuel a TV series. The key was to maintain what worked in the play. The phrase "comedy with heart" came up a lot. Once we explored and primed the world of the show, we challenged ourselves to write two scripts. We agreed on the stories, broke them down together, and individually wrote different episodes. Then we exchanged scripts and began to edit each other's words. This proved to be the most important part of our working relationship. This built trust and a common language. Writing is such a personal, private process. So intimate it's lonely at times. There were a few initial bumps, but we kept exchanging drafts until we forgot who wrote what. Thunderbird and Soulpepper read the scripts, gave their notes, and then, along with a document known as a "bible," which describes the world of the show, we submitted them to the CBC and eventually they said yes. They ordered two seasons, thirteen episodes a piece.

In the spring of 2015, Kevin and I read and interviewed many writers to staff the show. Then for two months in the fall, Anita Kapila, Garry Campbell, Sonja Bennett, Rebecca Kohler, along with Kevin and I, met across from the Art Gallery of Ontario in Strada Productions' third-floor office and brainstormed ideas, beat out stories, and wove them together. In January 2016, we assigned episodes to all the writers, including ourselves. Each episode went through a process of notes from Thunderbird, Soulpepper, and the CBC, with Kevin and I ultimately massaging the scripts here and there.

In the spring of 2016, we interviewed directors, assistant directors, production designers, directors of photography, editors, costume designers, hair and makeup, continuity people; we scouted locations, auditioned actors, and arrived at our team. On May 24 we moved into ShowLine Studios at 915 Lakeshore Blvd East, and on June 20 we began shooting.

It's Thursday, June 30, 2016, 10:30 a.m. I'm sitting on a real bed in a fake bedroom behind Peter Wellington, the director; Frazer Brown, the DOP; Liz Farrer, the first assistant director; Frank Gentile, the gaffer; and Donna Gardon, the continuity person. We're getting room tone. The whole crew is still and silent as Stephen Marian and Dennis Nicholson record the sound of the fake living room for about ten seconds. It's a quiet ritual amidst the bustle of life on set. It's my favourite part of the day.

The most difficult part in all of this is creating — investing all your ego, personality, faith, energy, love, hope, and history —

and then loosening the grip of that creation just enough so others can get in and do what they do to what you've done. When it works, it's a collaborative miracle.

While the crew sets up between takes, I wander around the sets: the store, the apartment above the store, the car rental agency, Janet's bedroom, which, I imagine, used to be Jung's before Janet was born. And then they probably shared the room for a while — maybe even until he left home. Janet still has his skateboard, which sits in the corner of the room. John Dondertman, the production designer, and his team went to my parents' home and church to do a bunch of "authentic Korean" research. Wouldn't have had it any other way.

My wandering lands me outside. Lakeshore Blvd East isn't the most inspirational view, but I look up and it's all sky. A dome of scratches and curls. Billowing clouds. Birds. Prayers. Blessings. Like a mustard seed that grows into a sheltering tree. And then I hear a voice: "I found Ins. Copy that." One of the assistant directors on her walkie-talkie kindly urges me to return to the set. "Sorry."

I'm making a TV show based on my play for the CBC, and I'm loving every moment.

ACKNOWLEDGEMENTS

No artist works in isolation. They stand on the shoulders of their predecessors and are sharpened by their peers. The following is a list of people who have helped me with this play artistically and financially. From an idea to the page to the stage to this book, thank you:

fu-GEN, Nina Lee-Aquino, David Yee, Richard Lee, K3, Joe Guno Park, Jovanni Sy, Grace Lynn Kung, Sean Baek, Dale Yim, Stephanie Jung, Kelly Park, Andrea Kwan, Benny Min, Silver Kim, Jo Chim, Ontario Arts Council, Toronto Arts Council, Diaspora Dialogues, Grace Toronto Church, Iris Turcott, Jason Rothery, Toby Malone, Consul General of the Republic of Korea, Hong Ji-In, Hyejeong Ahn, Myung Joon Park, Abraham Yi, Rich and Ed at Team RichKim, Bethel coffee house, Song Cook restaurant, Ian Liwanag, Jason and Mrs. Lee at Han Kuk Kwan restaurant, Sabina Song, Anne Purcell, Isa Palanca, Shinja Song, Jung and Janey Chee, Toronto Korean Bethel Church, Shen Young, David So, John Franklin, Rev. Dan MacDonald, Roger and Kevin Garland, Sam Cheng,

Katharine Kim, Derrick Chua, Gideon Arthur, Andrea Cross, Paul King, Aimee Lee, Jae Lee, Jamie Lee, Jacob Lee, Sara Purcell, Leo Purcell, Trinity Purcell, Elissa Purcell, Benjamin Purcell, Reverend Jin Sook Ko, Peter Lee, Young Ko, Rina Kim, Isabella Ko, Spencer Ko, Young Jong Ko, Anita Ko, Olivia Ko, William Ko, Andrew Ko, Shua Shin, Rev. Sam Shin, Charisa Shin, Sarah Shin, Elizabeth Shin, Jack Shin, Su Young Kim, Minjae Bae, Phineas Kim, Oliver Kim, Clark Choi, Sharon Choi, Esther Hyun, David Hyun, Emily Hyun, Hanna Hyun, Marcus Choi, Toyoung Kim, Sang Sill Kim, Suk Bong Ko, Sang Kil Ko, Roosevelt Cheh, Hyon Suk Choi, Kimi Yoshida, Adam Avitabile, Yuri Yoshida, Tatsu Takada, Tak and Fumi Yoshida, Anansi Press, Janie Yoon, Sarah MacLachlan, Soulpepper Theatre, Albert Schultz, Leslie Lester, Claire Sakaki, Weyni Mengesha, Ken Mackenzie, Thomas Ryder Pane, Lorenzo Savoini, Nancy Dryden, Sojeong Choi, Kat Chin, Leon Aureus, Andre Sills, Clé Bennett, Esther Jun, Jean Yoon, Paul Sun-Hyung Lee; my Umma, In-Heung Choi; my appa, Rev. Sang Bong Choi; my daughter, Poem; my son, River; and my amazing wife, Mari.

fu-gen.org
soulpepper.ca
houseofanansi.com
thunderbird.tv
cbc.ca
inschoi.com

INS CHOI is an actor and a playwright. His first play, *Kim's Convenience*, won Best New Play and was Patron's Pick at the 2011 Toronto Fringe Festival. The play then launched Soulpepper Theatre's 2012 season to a sold-out run and rave reviews. The play was adapted into a Canadian Screen Award–winning television series. Choi is also the creator of the one-person show *Subway Stations of the Cross*, which was published as a work of graphic poetry, with illustrations by Guno Park. Born in South Korea, Choi grew up in Scarborough, and now resides in Toronto with his lovely wife, Mari, and their two children, Poem and River.